apartment

house

SHACK

MANSION

house

apartment

MANSION

SHACK

house

ACK

apartment

house

MANSION

artment

se

SHACK

house

ON

partment

use

MANS

MANSION

SHACK

house

SHACK

MANSION

SHACK

apartment

house

SHACK

house

ON

artment

MANSION

MANSION

apart

SHACK

D1316185

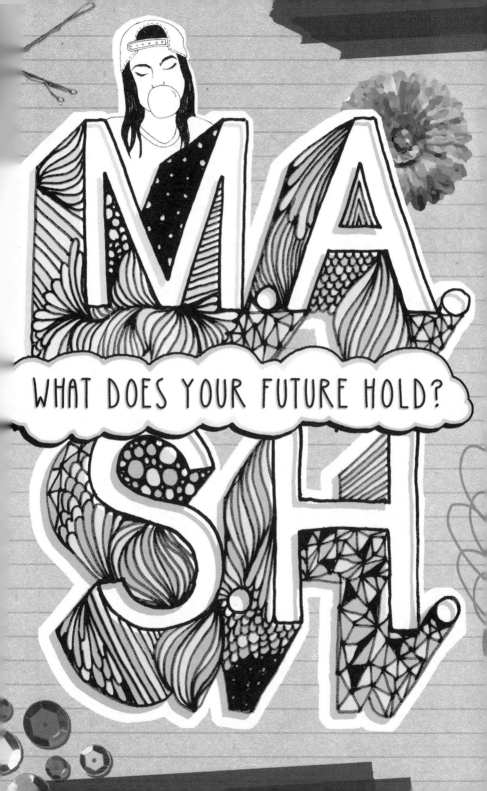

M.A.S.H.

WHAT DOES YOUR FUTURE HOLD?

STERLING CHILDREN'S BOOKS
New York

An Imprint of Sterling Publishing Co., Inc.
1166 Avenue of the Americas
New York, NY 10036

ISBN 978-1-4549-2278-0

Distributed in Canada by Sterling Publishing Co., Inc.
c/o Canadian Manda Group, 664 Annette Street
Toronto, Ontario, Canada M6S 2C8
Distributed in the United Kingdom by GMC Distribution Services
Castle Place, 166 High Street, Lewes, East Sussex, England BN7 1XU
Distributed in Australia by NewSouth Books
45 Beach Street, Coogee, NSW 2034, Australia

For information about custom editions, special sales, and premium and corporate purchases,
please contact Sterling Special Sales at 800-805-5489 or specialsales@sterlingpublishing.com.

Manufactured in Canada

Lot #:
2 4 6 8 10 9 7 5 3 1
03/17

www.sterlingpublishing.com

Line art by Bethany Robertson
Design by Ryan Thomann

CONTENTS

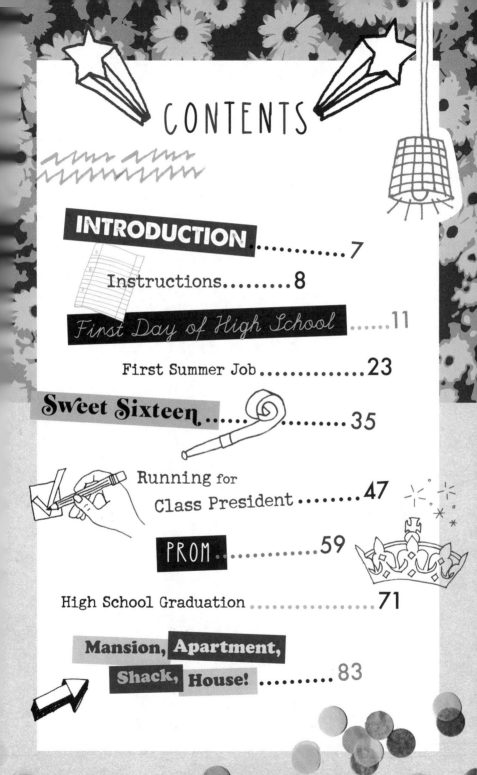

INTRODUCTION

MASH!

MANSION, *apartment,* **SHACK,** or **house**—which do you think you'll live in when you're older? What kind of **job** will you have? What kind of **car** will you drive?

ALL THAT ADULT STUFF is still far away, but it's fun to imagine what the future holds! Gather your friends for a game that predicts how your **prom** will go, where you'll throw the ultimate **sweet sixteen** birthday bash, and how you'll win the election for **class president!**

INSTRUCTIONS

WHAT YOU NEED:

- A pen or pencil
- A sense of humor

HOW THE GAME WORKS:

Read each question out loud and have your friend offer three possible answers. She cannot choose the same answer twice—that would be cheating! Jot the answers down in the blanks provided. Here's the fun part—you get to choose what goes in the fourth blank! Are you going to predict something nice for your friend's future or not? (Hint: The stranger the choices, the more interesting the results!)

Here's where it gets a liiiiittle complicated— when all the blanks are filled in, flip to the back side of the page and have your friend close her eyes. Draw a swirl in the space provided. Keep drawing until your friend says "Stop!" Draw a diagonal line through the middle of the swirl, and count all the places where the

8

line and the swirl intersect. Write this magic number down in the space provided.

Let's say your magic number is 6. Flip back to the previous page and count every answer choice starting from the top until you reach six. Cross that sixth option out, and start the count over on the next available answer choice.

Continue to eliminate every sixth choice as you move through the questions. When you reach the end of the page, continue the count at the beginning, starting from whichever number you left off on. Remember, once an answer choice has been crossed out, it can no longer be counted in the elimination process. Skip over it as you count. When there's only one answer choice left in a category, circle that option, and skip over that entire category as you keep counting.

Continue this process of elimination until one answer choice is circled in each category. Read the results out loud to your friend. Then swap places with her, so you can figure out your future, too!

First Day of High School

It's the **first day** of the rest of your life. The next four years are going to be a crazy-fun journey—if only you can get off to a good start.

First Day of HIGH SCHOOL

First Day of High School

What outfit do you wear?

1. _____
2. _____
3. _____
4. _____

Which after-school club do you join?

1. _____
2. _____
3. _____
4. _____

How is your hair done?

1. _____
2. _____
3. _____
4. _____

Who is your instant crush?

1. _____
2. _____
3. _____
4. _____

How do you get to school?

1. _____
2. _____
3. _____
4. _____

How many new friends do you make?

1. _____
2. _____
3. _____
4. _____

Who do you sit with at lunch?

1. _____
2. _____
3. _____
4. _____

GOOD LUCK!

MAGIC
NUMBER: _____

What outfit do you wear?

1. _____
2. _____
3. _____
4. _____

How is your hair done?

1. _____
2. _____
3. _____
4. _____

Which after-school club do you join?

1. _____
2. _____
3. _____
4. _____

How do you get to school?

1. _____
2. _____
3. _____
4. _____

Who is your instant crush?

1. _____
2. _____
3. _____
4. _____

Who do you sit with at lunch?

1. _____
2. _____
3. _____
4. _____

How many new friends do you make?

1. _____
2. _____
3. _____
4. _____

MAGIC NUMBER: _____

First Day of High School

What outfit do you wear?

1. ....
2. ....
3. ....
4. ....

How is your hair done?

1. ....
2. ....
3. ....
4. ....

Which after-school club do you join?

1. ....
2. ....
3. ....
4. ....

How do you get to school?

1. ....
2. ....
3. ....
4. ....

Who is your instant crush?

1. ....
2. ....
3. ....
4. ....

Who do you sit with at lunch?

1. ....
2. ....
3. ....
4. ....

How many new friends do you make?

1. ....
2. ....
3. ....
4. ....

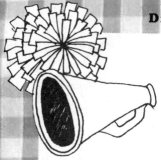

Magic
Number:

. . . .

What outfit do you wear?

1.
2.
3.
4.

Which after-school club do you join?

1.
2.
3.
4.

How is your hair done?

1.
2.
3.
4.

Who is your instant crush?

1.
2.
3.
4.

How do you get to school?

1.
2.
3.
4.

How many new friends do you make?

1.
2.
3.
4.

Who do you sit with at lunch?

1.
2.
3.
4.

Magic Number: _____

What outfit
do you wear?

1. _____
2. _____
3. _____
4. _____

How is your
hair done?

1. _____
2. _____
3. _____
4. _____

Which after-school
club do you join?

1. _____
2. _____
3. _____
4. _____

How do you
get to school?

1. _____
2. _____
3. _____
4. _____

Who is your
instant crush?

1. _____
2. _____
3. _____
4. _____

Who do you sit with
at lunch?

1. _____
2. _____
3. _____
4. _____

How many new friends
do you make?

1. _____
2. _____
3. _____
4. _____

MAGIC
NUMBER:

_____

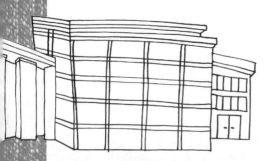

First Summer Job

It's time to take on some responsibility and start saving up—but will a scary boss or a dinky workplace turn your summer into a bummer?

First Summer Job

Where do you work?

1. _____
2. _____
3. _____
4. _____

How much do you make an hour?

1. _____
2. _____
3. _____
4. _____

Someone you know is working with you! Who is it?

1. _____
2. _____
3. _____
4. _____

Who is your boss?

1. _____
2. _____
3. _____
4. _____

What do you do when you're NOT working?

1. _____
2. _____
3. _____
4. _____

By the end of summer, how much money have you saved?

1. _____
2. _____
3. _____
4. _____

What do you do with your earnings?

1. _____
2. _____
3. _____
4. _____

MAGIC
NUMBER: _____

Where do you work?

1.
2.
3.
4.

How much do you make an hour?

1.
2.
3.
4.

What do you do when you're NOT working?

1.
2.
3.
4.

Someone you know is working with you! Who is it?

1.
2.
3.
4.

By the end of summer, how much money have you saved?

1.
2.
3.
4.

Who is your boss?

1.
2.
3.
4.

What do you do with your earnings?

1.
2.
3.
4.

MAGIC
NUMBER: _____

Where do you work?

1. ....
2. ....
3. ....
4. ....

How much do you make an hour?

1. ....
2. ....
3. ....
4. ....

What do you do when you're NOT working?

1. ....
2. ....
3. ....
4. ....

Someone you know is working with you! Who is it?

1. ....
2. ....
3. ....
4. ....

By the end of summer, how much money have you saved?

1. ....
2. ....
3. ....
4. ....

Who is your boss?

1. ....
2. ....
3. ....
4. ....

What do you do with your earnings?

1. ....
2. ....
3. ....
4. ....

Magic
Number:

....

Where do you work?

1.
2.
3.
4.

What do you do when you're NOT working?

1.
2.
3.
4.

How much do you make an hour?

1.
2.
3.
4.

By the end of summer, how much money have you saved?

1.
2.
3.
4.

Someone you know is working with you! Who is it?

1.
2.
3.
4.

What do you do with your earnings?

1.
2.
3.
4.

Who is your boss?

1.
2.
3.
4.

Magic Number: ~~~~~~~~~~~~~

Where do
you work?

1. _____
2. _____
3. _____
4. _____

How much do
you make an hour?

1. _____
2. _____
3. _____
4. _____

What do you do when
you're NOT working?

1. _____
2. _____
3. _____
4. _____

Someone you know is working
with you! Who is it?

1. _____
2. _____
3. _____
4. _____

By the end of summer, how
much money have you saved?

1. _____
2. _____
3. _____
4. _____

Who is
your boss?

1. _____
2. _____
3. _____
4. _____

What do you do with
your earnings?

1. _____
2. _____
3. _____
4. _____

MAGIC
NUMBER:

_____

Sweet Sixteen

This party could be the bash of the century—unless something goes wrong. Will your sweet sixteen be magical or an absolute mess?

Where do you host your party?

1. _____
2. _____
3. _____
4. _____

How many people attend?

1. _____
2. _____
3. _____
4. _____

What do you wear?

1. _____
2. _____
3. _____
4. _____

What is your birthday wish?

1. _____
2. _____
3. _____
4. _____

What hit song does everyone dance to?

1. _____
2. _____
3. _____
4. _____

What is the best present you receive?

1. _____
2. _____
3. _____
4. _____

What kind of cake do you have?

1. _____
2. _____
3. _____
4. _____

MAGIC
NUMBER: _____

Where do you host your party?

1. _____
2. _____
3. _____
4. _____

How many people attend?

1. _____
2. _____
3. _____
4. _____

What is your birthday wish?

1. _____
2. _____
3. _____
4. _____

What do you wear?

1. _____
2. _____
3. _____
4. _____

What hit song does everyone dance to?

1. _____
2. _____
3. _____
4. _____

What kind of cake do you have?

1. _____
2. _____
3. _____
4. _____

What is the best present you receive?

1. _____
2. _____
3. _____
4. _____

MAGIC NUMBER: _____

Sweet Sixteen

Where do you host your party?

1. ....
2. ....
3. ....
4. ....

How many people attend?

1. ....
2. ....
3. ....
4. ....

What is your birthday wish?

1. ....
2. ....
3. ....
4. ....

What do you wear?

1. ....
2. ....
3. ....
4. ....

What hit song does everyone dance to?

1. ....
2. ....
3. ....
4. ....

What kind of cake do you have?

1. ....
2. ....
3. ....
4. ....

What is the best present you receive?

1. ....
2. ....
3. ....
4. ....

**Magic
Number:**

....

Where do you host your party?

1.
2.
3.
4.

What is your birthday wish?

1.
2.
3.
4.

How many people attend?

1.
2.
3.
4.

What hit song does everyone dance to?

1.
2.
3.
4.

What do you wear?

1.
2.
3.
4.

What is the best present you receive?

1.
2.
3.
4.

What kind of cake do you have?

1.
2.
3.
4.

Magic Number: _____

Where do you
host your party?

1. _____

2. _____

3. _____

4. _____

How many
people attend?

1. _____

2. _____

3. _____

4. _____

What do
you wear?

1. _____

2. _____

3. _____

4. _____

What kind of cake
do you have?

1. _____

2. _____

3. _____

4. _____

What is your
birthday wish?

1. _____

2. _____

3. _____

4. _____

What hit song does
everyone dance to?

1. _____

2. _____

3. _____

4. _____

What is the best
present you receive?

1. _____

2. _____

3. _____

4. _____

※ MAGIC ※
NUMBER:

_____

Running for Class President

As class president, it's your job to make the school a better place. How will you organize your campaign to prove that you're ready for this leadership role?

CAST YOUR BALLOT

VOTE

VOTE

VOTE

★ class ★
ELECTION
. . . .

Running for Class President

What's your campaign slogan?

1. _____
2. _____
3. _____
4. _____

Who's your main opponent?

1. _____
2. _____
3. _____
4. _____

Who's your running mate?

1. _____
2. _____
3. _____
4. _____

You win the election! How many people voted for you?

1. _____
2. _____
3. _____
4. _____

What colors are your posters?

1. _____
2. _____
3. _____
4. _____

What's the first big decision you make?

1. _____
2. _____
3. _____
4. _____

What campaign promise do you make?

1. _____
2. _____
3. _____
4. _____

BALLOTS

MAGIC
NUMBER: _____

What's your campaign slogan?

1. _____
2. _____
3. _____
4. _____

Who's your running mate?

1. _____
2. _____
3. _____
4. _____

Who's your main opponent?

1. _____
2. _____
3. _____
4. _____

What colors are your posters?

1. _____
2. _____
3. _____
4. _____

You win the election! How many people voted for you?

1. _____
2. _____
3. _____
4. _____

What campaign promise do you make?

1. _____
2. _____
3. _____
4. _____

What's the first big decision you make?

1. _____
2. _____
3. _____
4. _____

✓ ✓
MAGIC ✓
NUMBER: _____
✓

What's your campaign slogan?

1. ....
2. ....
3. ....
4. ....

Who's your running mate?

1. ....
2. ....
3. ....
4. ....

Who's your main opponent?

1. ....
2. ....
3. ....
4. ....

What colors are your posters?

1. ....
2. ....
3. ....
4. ....

You win the election! How many people voted for you?

1. ....
2. ....
3. ....
4. ....

What campaign promise do you make?

1. ....
2. ....
3. ....
4. ....

What's the first big decision you make?

1. ....
2. ....
3. ....
4. ....

Magic
Number:

....

What's your campaign slogan?

1. 〰〰〰〰〰〰〰〰〰〰
2. 〰〰〰〰〰〰〰〰〰〰
3. 〰〰〰〰〰〰〰〰〰〰
4. 〰〰〰〰〰〰〰〰〰〰

Who's your main opponent?

1. 〰〰〰〰〰〰〰〰〰〰
2. 〰〰〰〰〰〰〰〰〰〰
3. 〰〰〰〰〰〰〰〰〰〰
4. 〰〰〰〰〰〰〰〰〰〰

Who's your running mate?

1. 〰〰〰〰〰〰〰〰〰〰
2. 〰〰〰〰〰〰〰〰〰〰
3. 〰〰〰〰〰〰〰〰〰〰
4. 〰〰〰〰〰〰〰〰〰〰

You win the election! How many people voted for you?

1. 〰〰〰〰〰〰〰〰〰〰
2. 〰〰〰〰〰〰〰〰〰〰
3. 〰〰〰〰〰〰〰〰〰〰
4. 〰〰〰〰〰〰〰〰〰〰

What colors are your posters?

1. 〰〰〰〰〰〰〰〰〰〰
2. 〰〰〰〰〰〰〰〰〰〰
3. 〰〰〰〰〰〰〰〰〰〰
4. 〰〰〰〰〰〰〰〰〰〰

What's the first big decision you make?

1. 〰〰〰〰〰〰〰〰〰〰
2. 〰〰〰〰〰〰〰〰〰〰
3. 〰〰〰〰〰〰〰〰〰〰
4. 〰〰〰〰〰〰〰〰〰〰

What campaign promise do you make?

1. 〰〰〰〰〰〰〰〰〰〰
2. 〰〰〰〰〰〰〰〰〰〰
3. 〰〰〰〰〰〰〰〰〰〰
4. 〰〰〰〰〰〰〰〰〰〰

VOTE VOTE

Magic Number: ～～～～～

What's your
campaign slogan?

1. _____
2. _____
3. _____
4. _____

Every VOTE counts!

Who's your
running mate?

1. _____
2. _____
3. _____
4. _____

Who's your
main opponent?

1. _____
2. _____
3. _____
4. _____

What colors are
your posters?

1. _____
2. _____
3. _____
4. _____

You win the election! How
many people voted for you?

1. _____
2. _____
3. _____
4. _____

What campaign promise
do you make?

1. _____
2. _____
3. _____
4. _____

What's the first big decision
you make as class president?

1. _____
2. _____
3. _____
4. _____

MAGIC
NUMBER:

_____

Prom

It's the most glamorous event of your high school career, and senior year would be totally lame without it. Will prom be as perfect as you've always imagined?

What's the theme of the dance?

1. _____
2. _____
3. _____
4. _____

Who's your date?

1. _____
2. _____
3. _____
4. _____

What color is your dress?

1. _____
2. _____
3. _____
4. _____

What flower is your corsage made out of?

1. _____
2. _____
3. _____
4. _____

What song do you and your date slow dance to?

1. _____
2. _____
3. _____
4. _____

Who is crowned prom king?

1. _____
2. _____
3. _____
4. _____

Who is crowned prom queen?

1. _____
2. _____
3. _____
4. _____

MAGIC
NUMBER: _____

What's the theme
of the dance?

1. _____

2. _____

3. _____

4. _____

QUEEN

Who's your date?

1. _____

2. _____

3. _____

4. _____

What song do you and
your date slow dance to?

1. _____

2. _____

3. _____

4. _____

What color
is your dress?

1. _____

2. _____

3. _____

4. _____

Who is crowned
prom king?

1. _____

2. _____

3. _____

4. _____

What flower is your
corsage made out of?

1. _____

2. _____

3. _____

4. _____

Who is crowned
prom queen?

1. _____

2. _____

3. _____

4. _____

MAGIC NUMBER: _____

Let's DANCE

What's the theme
of the dance?

1. ....
2. ....
3. ....
4. ....

PROM

**What song do you
and your date
slow dance to?**

1. ....
2. ....
3. ....
4. ....

Who's your date?

1. ....
2. ....
3. ....
4. ....

**What color
is your dress?**

1. ....
2. ....
3. ....
4. ....

**Who is crowned
prom king?**

1. ....
2. ....
3. ....
4. ....

**What flower is your
corsage made out of?**

1. ....
2. ....
3. ....
4. ....

**Who is crowned
prom queen?**

1. ....
2. ....
3. ....
4. ....

Magic
Number:

What's the theme of the dance?

1.
2.
3.
4.

What song do you and your date slow dance to?

1.
2.
3.
4.

Who's your date?

1.
2.
3.
4.

Who is crowned prom king?

1.
2.
3.
4.

What color is your dress?

1.
2.
3.
4.

Who is crowned prom queen?

1.
2.
3.
4.

What flower is your corsage made out of?

1.
2.
3.
4.

KING

Magic Number: _____

What's the theme
of the dance?

1. _____
2. _____
3. _____
4. _____

Who's
your date?

1. _____
2. _____
3. _____
4. _____

What song do you and
your date slow dance to?

1. _____
2. _____
3. _____
4. _____

What color
is your dress?

1. _____
2. _____
3. _____
4. _____

Who is crowned
prom king?

1. _____
2. _____
3. _____
4. _____

What flower is your
corsage made out of?

1. _____
2. _____
3. _____
4. _____

Who is crowned
prom queen?

1. _____
2. _____
3. _____
4. _____

MAGIC NUMBER:

High School Graduation

With a diploma in hand, the world is yours to conquer. Just make sure you keep your high school besties by your side. How does this big day go down?

What color is your graduation robe?

1.
2.
3.
4.

What do you get as a graduation gift?

1.
2.
3.
4.

What outfit do you wear under your robe?

1.
2.
3.
4.

How many parties do you attend?

1.
2.
3.
4.

What's the last sentence in your graduation speech?

1.
2.
3.
4.

How do you spend the summer after graduation?

1.
2.
3.
4.

Who hugs you first after the ceremony?

1.
2.
3.
4.

MAGIC
NUMBER: _____

What color is your
graduation robe?

1. _____

2. _____

3. _____

4. _____

CONGRATS!

What outfit do you
wear under your robe?

1. _____

2. _____

3. _____

4. _____

What do you get
as a graduation gift?

1. _____

2. _____

3. _____

4. _____

What's the last sentence in
your graduation speech?

1. _____

2. _____

3. _____

4. _____

How many parties
do you attend?

1. _____

2. _____

3. _____

4. _____

Who hugs you first
after the ceremony?

1. _____

2. _____

3. _____

4. _____

How do you spend the
summer after graduation?

1. _____

2. _____

3. _____

4. _____

YOU
DID
IT!

MAGIC
NUMBER: _____

What color is your graduation robe?

1. ....
2. ....
3. ....
4. ....

What outfit do you wear under your robe?

1. ....
2. ....
3. ....
4. ....

What do you get as a graduation gift?

1. ....
2. ....
3. ....
4. ....

What's the last sentence in your graduation speech?

1. ....
2. ....
3. ....
4. ....

How many parties do you attend?

1. ....
2. ....
3. ....
4. ....

Who hugs you first after the ceremony?

1. ....
2. ....
3. ....
4. ....

How do you spend the summer after graduation?

1. ....
2. ....
3. ....
4. ....

Magic
Number:

. . . .

What color is your graduation robe?

1. _____
2. _____
3. _____
4. _____

What do you get as a graduation gift?

1. _____
2. _____
3. _____
4. _____

What outfit do you wear under your robe?

1. _____
2. _____
3. _____
4. _____

How many parties do you attend?

1. _____
2. _____
3. _____
4. _____

What's the last sentence in your graduation speech?

1. _____
2. _____
3. _____
4. _____

How do you spend the summer after graduation?

1. _____
2. _____
3. _____
4. _____

Who hugs you first after the ceremony?

1. _____
2. _____
3. _____
4. _____

GOOD
LUCK!

Magic Number: ＿＿＿＿＿

What color is your graduation robe?

1.
2.
3.
4.

What outfit do you wear under your robe?

1.
2.
3.
4.

What do you get as a graduation gift?

1.
2.
3.
4.

What's the last sentence in your graduation speech?

1.
2.
3.
4.

How many parties do you attend?

1.
2.
3.
4.

Who hugs you first after the ceremony?

1.
2.
3.
4.

How do you spend the summer after graduation?

1.
2.
3.
4.

MAGIC
NUMBER:

_____

Mansion, Apartment, Shack, House!

Fast-forward wayyyy into the future. You're an adult now! What does your life look like?

happily
ever
after...

Mansion, Apartment, Shack, House!

Who are you married to?

1. _____
2. _____
3. _____
4. _____

What color is your wedding dress?

1. _____
2. _____
3. _____
4. _____

Which city do you live in?

1. _____
2. _____
3. _____
4. _____

What is your job?

1. _____
2. _____
3. _____
4. _____

What kind of car do you drive?

1. _____
2. _____
3. _____
4. _____

How many kids do you have?

1. _____
2. _____
3. _____
4. _____

What kind of home do you live in?

1. Mansion
2. Apartment
3. Shack
4. House

YAY!

MAGIC
NUMBER: _____

Who are you married to?

1. _____
2. _____
3. _____
4. _____

What color is your wedding dress?

1. _____
2. _____
3. _____
4. _____

What kind of car do you drive?

1. _____
2. _____
3. _____
4. _____

Which city do you live in?

1. _____
2. _____
3. _____
4. _____

How many kids do you have?

1. _____
2. _____
3. _____
4. _____

What is your job?

1. _____
2. _____
3. _____
4. _____

What kind of home do you live in?

1. Mansion
2. Apartment
3. Shack
4. House

MAGIC
NUMBER: _____

Who are you
married to?

1. ....
2. ....
3. ....
4. ....

MASH

**What color is your
wedding dress?**

1. ....
2. ....
3. ....
4. ....

**What kind of car
do you drive?**

1. ....
2. ....
3. ....
4. ....

**Which city do
you live in?**

1. ....
2. ....
3. ....
4. ....

**How many kids
do you have?**

1. ....
2. ....
3. ....
4. ....

What is your job?

1. ....
2. ....
3. ....
4. ....

**What kind of home
do you live in?**

1. Mansion ....
2. Apartment ....
3. Shack ....
4. House

Magic ✶
Number:

. . . .

Who are you married to?

1.
2.
3.
4.

What kind of car do you drive?

1.
2.
3.
4.

What color is your wedding dress?

1.
2.
3.
4.

How many kids do you have?

1.
2.
3.
4.

Which city do you live in?

1.
2.
3.
4.

What kind of home do you live in?

1. Mansion
2. Apartment
3. Shack
4. House

What is your job?

1.
2.
3.
4.

Magic Number: ﹏﹏﹏﹏﹏

Who are you
married to?

1.
2.
3.
4.

**What color is your
wedding dress?**

1.
2.
3.
4.

**Which city do
you live in?**

1.
2.
3.
4.

**What is
your job?**

1.
2.
3.
4.

**What kind of car
do you drive?**

1.
2.
3.
4.

**How many kids
do you have?**

1.
2.
3.
4.

**What kind of home
do you live in?**

1. Mansion
2. Apartment
3. Shack
4. House

MAGIC
NUMBER:

_____

ℐNow that you're a pro

at M.A.S.H., you can create your own game.
Here's how:

1. Choose a **topic** (something about the future,
like first car or first vacation with friends).

2. Think of some **questions** related to
that topic (as many as you want!).

3. Write the **questions** on a piece of paper,
leaving space for answer choices (the number
of answer choices allowed is up to you!).

ET VOILÁ!—a totally original game for you and
your friends to play.

The **future** is **unpredictable.**

The **possibilities**
are **endless.**

Let the fun
and games begin!

apartment
house
SHACK
house
MANSION
MANSION
SHACK
house
apartment
house
apartment
SHACK
MANSION
apartment
SHACK
house
MANSION
apartment
SHACK
house
MANSION
SHACK
apartment
house
MANSION
SHACK
house
MANSION